Mostly Happy! CLIP ART

OF THE THIRTIES, FORTIES & FIFTIES

SELECTED & EDITED BY JERRY JANKOWSKI

The **ILLUSTRATIONS** and **ADVERTISEMENTS** contained in this book were compiled from original ad cut/clip art catalogs and magazines of the **THIRTIES**, **FORTIES** and **FIFTIES**. These **UPBEAT** and slightly **QUIRKY** works reflect the sensibilities of the times—the economic hardships of the thirties, the war years of the forties and the unbridled optimism and prosperity of the fifties. Companies used these "spot" illustrations, which were created largely by anonymous **COMMERCIAL ARTISTS**, to enliven business cards, guest checks, matchbook covers, advertising and editorial works.

Unlike most clip-art books, this collection contains **NO VICTORIAN** or early **ART DECO** filler. The items are also printed on good **QUALITY** stock, so that they can be **CLEANLY** enlarged. The crisp printing will be appreciated by anyone using a desktop scanner.

Examples of **SCANNED ART** appear on the first page of each of the 15 chapters. Scanned in at 300 dpi (dots per inch) using a line art setting and then imported into QuarkXPress, they have been greatly enlarged to show a handsome, **ROUGH-TEXTURED** outline. Some are further **DISTORTED** by inputting uneven values for the x% and y% box coordinates.

If you're looking for a specific image such as a **COCKTAIL GLASS**, **BUCKING BRONCO** or **TOASTER**, turn to the **INDEX**. But if it's just inspiration or ideas that you're looking for—**HAPPY BROWSING!**

ART DIRECTION BOOK CO., INC.

PUBLISHED BY:

ART DIRECTION BOOK CO., INC.

456 GLENBROOK ROAD • GLENBROOK, CT 06906

P: (203) 353-1441 F: (203) 353-1371

TABLE OF CONTENTS

MAINLY GUYS

Happy!

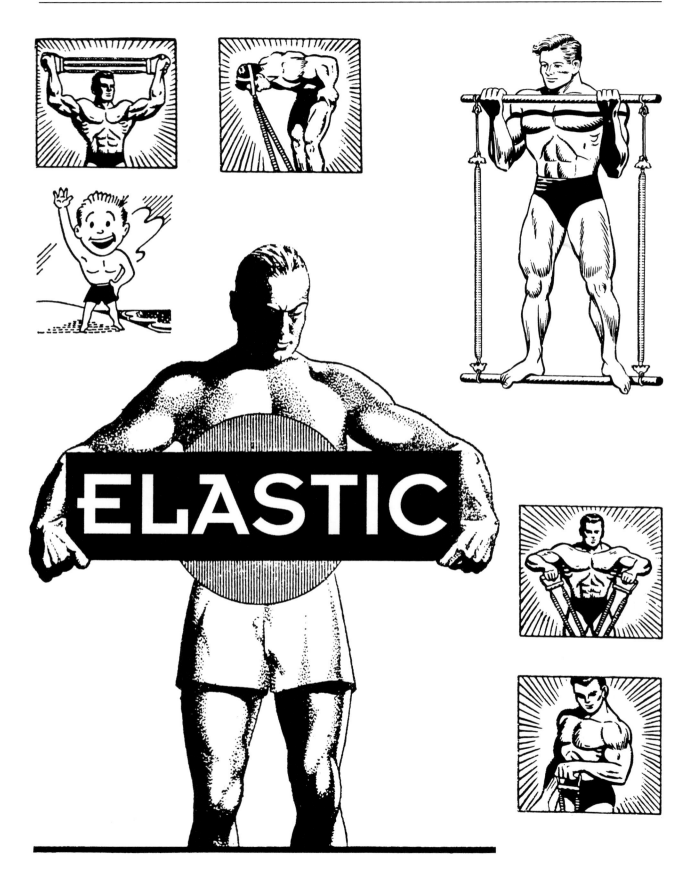

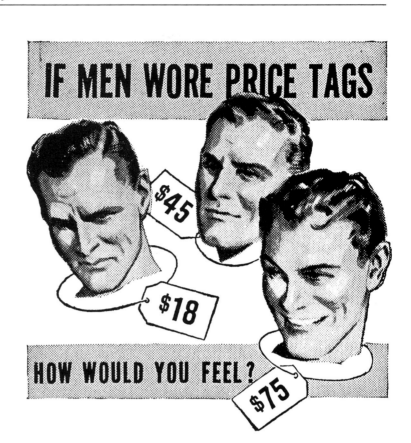

IF MEN WORE PRICE TAGS

$45

$18

HOW WOULD YOU FEEL?

$75

GOOD BODY BUILDER

LADIES & GENTS

SALE!

DRAFTING & DRAWING

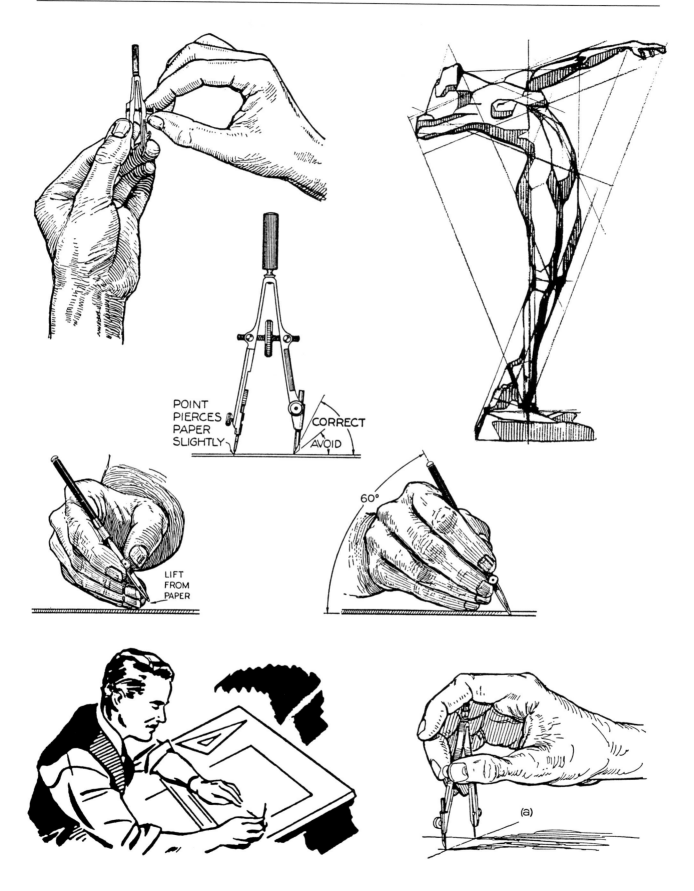

POINT
PIERCES
PAPER
SLIGHTLY

CORRECT

AVOID

LIFT
FROM
PAPER

60°

(a)

LOOKING GOOD

Dude Up

Doll Up

Dress up

TAILOR

Cleaning
Pressing
Repairing

we Shine

We Shine

HOME COOKING

New Recipes

EATING OUT

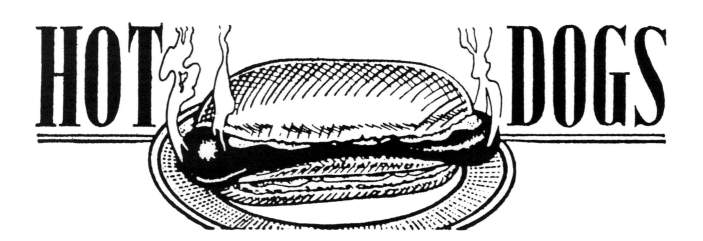

Eat with us Tonight — and Save
WE SERVE Good **food**
In a pleasant
Homey Atmosphere

Excellent **food.**
UNSURPASSED SERVICE
AN ATMOSPHERE YOU'LL LIKE

HAMBURGERS
with all the
TRIMMINGS

HAPPY HOUR

THE SPORTING LIFE

PUBLIC FEE COURSE

WE CATER TO TOURNAMENTS PRIVATE AND SPECIAL PARTIES

SPINNING FLY

SAVE
STEPS, TIME and TIRES

BON VOYAGE

WEST WAYS

Make Your Own
WESTERN BELT

Sky High!
in the Canadian Pacific Rockies

COLOMBIA

MEXICO

GUATEMALA

PANAMA

EL SALVADOR

WAR & PEACE

ODDS & ENDS

KEEP SMILING

INDEX

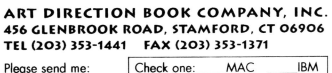